Picture of Evil

DOUBLE FASTBACK® *Spy*

Picture of Evil

JANET LORIMER

GLOBE FEARON
Pearson Learning Group

DOUBLE FASTBACK® SPY BOOKS

Against the Wall
The Black Gold Conspiracy
Claw the Cold, Cold Earth
A Dangerous Game
Escape From East Berlin

The Last Red Rose
Picture of Evil
The Puppeteer
The Race to Ross
The Silver Spy

All photography © Pearson Education, Inc. (PEI) unless specifically noted.

Copyright © 2004 by Pearson Education, Inc., publishing as Globe Fearon®, an imprint of Pearson Learning Group, 299 Jefferson Road, Parsippany, NJ 07054. All rights reserved. No part of this book may be reproduced or transmitted in any form or by any means, electronic or mechanical, including photocopying, recording, or by any information storage and retrieval system, without permission in writing from the publisher. For information regarding permission(s), write to Rights and Permissions Department.

Globe Fearon® and Fastback® are registered trademarks of Globe Fearon, Inc.

ISBN 0-13-024624-7
Printed in the United States of America
1 2 3 4 5 6 7 8 9 10   07 06 05 04 03

1-800-321-3106
www.pearsonlearning.com

Scott Gardner stopped halfway up Nob Hill to shift his camera bag from one shoulder to the other. He was breathing hard because the hill was steep and Scott had been walking fast. But he liked the exercise. It always felt good to stretch his muscles.

For a moment Scott rested, turning to look at the view of the city. He never got tired of the sights in San Francisco. It was the most beautiful city in the world, he thought. And there was always something exciting to see and photograph.

Today was a perfect day for walking in the city. The sun was bright, the sky was clear, and there was a stiff breeze blowing in from the bay. It was just the kind of day Scott loved.

He turned to look up the hill at his photography assignment for the day: The Mark Hopkins Hotel. It was one of the famous old hotels in San Francisco, and Scott was looking forward to taking pictures there. He took a deep breath and continued up the hill toward the hotel.

Scott worked as a photograhper for *San Francisco Leisure,* a magazine aimed mostly at tourists. He had worked for the magazine for nearly three years, and he loved his job. Of course, there were times when he wished he worked for one of the big news magazines. One of these days, Scott promised himself, he'd be on the spot to photograph a big event, something that would make national news! That picture would make him famous.

As he walked into the lobby of the Mark Hopkins, Scott grinned to himself. Getting that important picture was his favorite daydream. In the meantime, he had a job to do, and he'd better get busy.

Scott stopped in the middle of the hotel's lobby and looked around. His well-trained eyes were trying to find the best camera angles and the proper light.

As Scott looked around, he saw that the gift shop was just opening. His friend, Jason Roberts, was behind the counter unlocking the cash register. Scott decided to say hello to Jason before he began taking his pictures.

"Hey, Jason, how are you?" Scott said as he walked into the shop. Jason smiled and tipped his head to one side. Even though Jason was blind, his hearing was excellent. He recognized Scott's voice right away.

"Scott! What are you doing here?" Jason asked. Scott told Jason about his assignment to photograph the old San Francisco hotels for a magazine article. Jason listened closely, nodding now and then.

The blind man was in his late fifties. He was a large man with broad shoulders and a dark curly beard. Jason had not always been blind. At one time, he had worked as an agent for the CIA. Once in a while Scott could get Jason to tell him some of the exciting stories from his years as a government spy.

But there was one story Jason never talked about. That was the accident that had left him blind eight years ago. Scott knew that something terrible had happened while Jason was on an important operation. But Jason never went into any details about it.

When Scott finished talking about his photo assignment, he said, "By the way, if you're free tonight, how about joining

Trudy and me for dinner? There's a new restaurant we want to try."

Jason grinned. "That depends," he said. "If it's one of those fancy places that serves gourmet food, count me out. You know I'm a meat-and-potatoes man, Scott."

Scott laughed. "Actually, it's an Italian place. How do you feel about spaghetti?"

"Now that sounds good," Jason said. "What time?"

While they worked out the details, Scott noticed that the gift shop was beginning to fill up. A businessman in a gray suit was looking for a newspaper. A woman in a wide-brimmed yellow hat began to browse through the post cards. And a young couple holding hands strolled in. Scott grinned to himself. They looked like newlyweds on their honeymoon. They were far more interested in each other than in anything in the shop.

"I'd better let you get back to work," Scott told Jason. "Looks like business will be good today."

"I'm glad of that," Jason said. "It will pay for that spaghetti dinner."

Just before he left, Scott bought a copy of the local newspaper. He was scanning the stories on the front page as he started for the door. He wasn't really paying attention to where he was going. He bumped into a tall soldier entering the shop. "Oh, sorry!" Scott said. The soldier pushed past him with a grunt.

Outside the shop, Scott stopped to finish reading the paper's lead story before he went to work. The story was about Malcolm Carruthers, a man Scott greatly admired.

Carruthers was a spokesman for peace. He had done something no one else had been able to do. He had worked out a truce between the countries at war in the Middle East. Everyone hoped that this cooling off period would lead to lasting peace in that troubled area of the world. Now Carruthers was coming to San Francisco to give a speech about his work. Scott wished he could take the time to see Carruthers in person and hear the speech.

When he finished reading the story, Scott looked at his watch. Time to get to work. He pulled his camera from the camera bag and checked the setting. Everything was ready. He raised the camera to his eye and looked through the lens.

Suddenly he heard a shout coming from the gift shop. He turned quickly, the camera still to his eye. Through the lens he saw Jason stagger backward. He seemed to have lost his balance. Jason's head struck the sharp corner of a shelf, and he fell to the floor.

Without really thinking about it, Scott had snapped several pictures of this scene. Just as Jason hit the floor, Scott raced into the shop.

The customers began to back away. Several of them ran out of the shop, but a few crowded around Jason. Scott dropped to the floor beside his friend. Jason was trying to say something. Scott leaned close to hear.

"Stop him!" Jason whispered. "Stop blackbird." Then he passed out.

The hotel manager had come into the shop. He knelt down next to Scott. "I've called an ambulance," he said, "And the hotel doctor is on his way."

Scott turned to look at the people standing behind him. "Did any of you see what happened?" he asked.

"It all happened so fast," someone said. "I think one of the customers accidently knocked something off a shelf. I don't know why, but that blind man seemed to go crazy. He started to shout, and he seemed to lose his sense of direction. He fell back against that shelf and hit his head."

At that moment the hotel doctor arrived. Scott stood up and moved away to give the doctor room. While the doctor gave Jason first aid, Scott frowned in thought. What had Jason meant by those strange words? Why had he said, "Stop blackbird?"

After Jason was taken to the hospital, Scott went back to the lobby to finish his work. He still had a job to do. Besides, there wasn't anything he could do for Jason by just standing around and worrying. But while he was taking the pictures he needed, he kept thinking about Jason's strange words. They made no sense to him at all.

After Scott finished his photo assignment, he spent the rest of the morning taking pictures in Golden Gate Park. He wanted to add some photos to his own private collection. Finally, he went back to his apartment.

The first thing Scott did was to set up his darkroom. He was anxious to develop the rolls of film he'd shot. He wanted to be sure the pictures that he'd taken of the hotel had turned out. But he was also curious about the pictures he'd shot when Jason had been injured. Maybe they would tell him something that would shed some light on Jason's strange words.

But when he had made the prints and studied them, Scott felt disappointed. He had a few good shots of Jason losing his balance and falling. Scott could see Jason's face clearly in the pictures. He'd also caught the expressions on the faces of some of the customers. But the pictures didn't tell Scott anything new.

After he glanced at the pictures one more time, Scott put them aside. He looked at his watch and noticed it was already after four o'clock. He'd gotten so involved developing the photos, he'd nearly forgotten that he had an early dinner date with his girlfriend, Trudy. He just had time to jump into the shower and get dressed before he had to meet her.

A little while later, as he was about to walk out the door, Scott thought about Jason again. He really wanted to know how his friend was doing. So he called the hospital. But the news was not good. Jason was still unconscious.

Scott hung up the phone, feeling down. It would be hard to enjoy the evening while Jason lay in the hospital. Trudy would also be upset when Scott told her what had happened. She cared for Jason as much as Scott did.

Before he left the apartment, Scott picked up one of the pictures of Jason falling and stuck it in his pocket. He planned to show it to Trudy, and tell her about Jason's strange words. Maybe she could help make some sense of them.

Trudy was waiting at the restaurant when Scott got there. She also worked for *San Francisco Leisure,* as a staff writer and editor. She and Scott had begun dating several months before. They had both joined the magazine at the same time and found that they shared a lot in common. Neither of them was originally from San Francisco, so they spent much of their time exploring their new home together.

Scott apologized for being late. After they had ordered their dinners, he told her what had happened to Jason. Then he pulled out the photo and showed it to her.

Trudy studied it, her eyes filled with worry. "Will Jason be all right?" she asked.

"I hope so," Scott said. "The doctor says it's too early to tell. Jason really got a bad blow on the head."

"I wonder what upset him so much," Trudy said. "I can't believe that a small accident in the shop would do that. After all, Jason has often talked about how careless people can be. He's even laughed about it. And he doesn't sell anything that is very rare or costly."

"I know," Scott said. "It doesn't make any sense to me either. And those words, 'Stop blackbird.' What would they have to do with something being knocked off a shelf?"

"Maybe you didn't hear him right," Trudy said.

"No, I'm sure that's what he said," Scott said.

"Maybe his mind was just wandering," Trudy said. "After all, that was a bad injury."

"Maybe so," Scott said. But he didn't sound convinced. They were both silent for a moment, studying the picture. Then Scott said, "I keep thinking that Jason used the word 'blackbird' like a name. First he said, 'Stop him.' Then he said, 'Stop blackbird.' You know, as if it were someone's name—or maybe a code name".

Trudy grinned. "Now you're beginning to sound like James Bond. What are you trying to do, turn this whole thing into a scene from a spy story?"

Scott laughed. "Hey, I'm the guy who takes pictures. You're the writer."

Trudy laughed, too. "Okay," she said. "You want a spy story? Well, here's one. Today I got to meet a real spy. Alan Carter."

"Who's he?" Scott asked.

"He used to work for the CIA," Trudy said. "Just like Jason did. Anyway, Carter retired about a year ago. And now he's decided to write a book about his career. He's traveling around the country giving speeches to get people interested in his book. I'm certain he'll succeed. He told some pretty wild stories about his years with the CIA. People really love that spy stuff, especially when the spy is a real person."

"How did you get to meet him?" Scott asked.

"He held a press conference this morning. He's in town to give a speech at San Francisco State University. And the reporters really ate up everything he had to say. Especially when he began dropping hints about having a lot of secret information about the inner workings of the CIA."

Scott raised one eyebrow. "Oh, really?"

Trudy nodded. "He wouldn't give much away. But he did mention a double agent who worked for the agency."

"I bet the agency won't appreciate having Carter air its 'dirty laundry' in public," Scott said. "Can he get away with that?"

"I don't know," Trudy said. "Of course, what he puts in the book may not turn out to be as exciting and secretive as he makes it sound. But those hints he's dropping sure sound juicy."

Scott sighed. "Boy, I'd like to hear him speak," he said. "And Malcolm Carruthers, too. That's the trouble with living in this town, Trudy. All the really interesting things seem to happen at the same time."

After dinner, Trudy went home to finish up a story that she had to turn in at work the next day. She asked Scott to call her if he learned of any changes in Jason's condition. He agreed, and said that if there were no changes, he'd talk to her the next day at work. Then he stopped to pick up the evening paper and went back to his own apartment.

The moment Scott unlocked his door and stepped into the apartment, he stopped dead in his tracks. He stared about the room in shock. Someone had broken in. His files had been opened, and photographs and negatives had been thrown all over the living room floor.

Suddenly Scott felt a cold chill run down his back. Was the intruder still in the apartment? He picked up a heavy vase to use as a weapon, and moved carefully from room to room. The apartment was empty. The intruder was gone. And nothing in the other rooms had been touched. Just his files and—

The darkroom! Scott groaned when he thought of all his expensive equipment. He hurried to see if any damage had been done in the darkroom. But he found that none of his equipment had been touched. Scott let out a sigh of relief. Then he saw that something *had* been taken. All the prints and negatives that he'd taken at the Mark Hopkins that morning were gone.

The only picture he had left of that day's work was the one in his pocket. He pulled it out and stared at it. Why had the intruder been so interested in those pictures? Were any other photos missing? Scott hurried back to the living room and began to pick up the pictures and negatives on the floor. They were in such a mess that it was hard to tell if anything else was missing. But after sorting things out for a few moments, it looked to Scott as if nothing else had been taken. Just the film he'd shot that day at the hotel.

Scott knew right away what this meant. The scene in the gift shop hadn't been just an accident. Something else had been going on. And it was important enough for someone to commit a crime in order to erase any evidence of it. And that also meant that Jason's strange words had special meaning, too.

Scott hurried to the phone to call Trudy. He wanted her to know that he hadn't been imagining things after all. Just as he reached for the phone, it rang.

The moment he said hello, he heard Trudy's voice. She sounded scared and shaken. "Scott! Scott, I—"

Her voice was cut off in the middle of the sentence. Another voice came on the line. It was a gruff, deep male voice. "I have your girlfriend," the man said. "Right now she's okay, and she'll be okay as long as you do what I tell you. But if you don't—"

Scott's mouth went dry with fear. It didn't take much imagination to figure out that the kidnapper meant business.

"What do you want?" Scott asked.

"The photograph. The one you took this morning. You know the one I mean."

"But you've already taken all the prints and negatives of—"

"One of the prints is missing," the man said. "You must have it with you."

Scott thought quickly. The kidnapper had already taken some big risks to try to get that picture. So he must be desperate. If Scott gave it up, he would be losing the only clue he had to whatever had happened in the gift shop. On the other hand, the kidnapper had Trudy. He probably wouldn't think twice about killing her if he didn't get his hands on what he wanted. There was only one thing Scott could do. He had to make a copy of that picture before he turned it over to the kidnapper. But he needed time to do that. And he didn't want the kidnapper to figure out what he was doing.

"The photo isn't with me," Scott said. "I dropped it off at my magazine's office. I'll have to go get it first."

"You've got a half hour," the kidnapper said. "And don't try any smart stuff. The girl and I are leaving her apartment. So don't bother calling the police. Understand?"

"I understand," Scott said. His heart was pounding and his hands were cold and damp. "Where do I bring the photo?"

"Golden Gate Park," the kidnapper said. "You know where the handball courts are? That's where we'll be. But remember, if I see the cops, the girl is dead."

"No cops," Scott promised. "But you've got to give me more than a half hour. The magazine office is on the other side of town."

There was a moment of silence while the kidnapper thought this over. Then he said, "Okay, you've got an hour. But that's it!"

"I'll be there," Scott said.

Suddenly there was a click. The kidnapper had hung up. Scott took a deep breath. It had worked. The man had bought his story. Scott would have enough time to make the copy and get to the park. But he knew he was cutting it awfully close.

Scott hurried to the darkroom. He knew he had to be as calm as possible because this was delicate work. He couldn't afford to let his hands shake. He tried to put the sound of Trudy's frightened voice out of his mind.

At last the job was done. Using the developed photo, Scott had made a fresh negative. But he didn't have time to develop it now. That would have to wait until Trudy was safe. Scott grabbed the print, turned off his photo equipment, and left his apartment.

Twenty minutes later, Scott parked his car in Golden Gate Park in front of Steinhart Aquarium. Then he crossed the street to the handball courts.

The courts were empty. Scott looked nervously at his watch. He was a few minutes late. He hoped the kidnapper hadn't gotten impatient and hurt Trudy.

Suddenly a man's deep voice caught him by surprise. It came from a small grove of trees nearby. "Stop right there!" Scott stopped. "Take out the photo," the voice ordered. "Now put it on the ground, and back away from it," the man went on.

Trudy and the kidnapper stepped out of the shadows. The man was wearing a hat pulled down low. A nylon stocking masked his features. And he was wearing a large overcoat that hid his size and shape.

Trudy's arms were bound behind her back and there was tape over her mouth. Her eyes were wide with fear.

The kidnapper pushed Trudy ahead of him. When he got to the picture, he leaned down and picked it up. For a moment he studied it closely. Then he gave Trudy a push toward Scott. She staggered and almost fell, but Scott caught her in time. At the same time, the kidnapper turned and ran for the trees. The shadows swallowed him.

Scott untied Trudy's wrists and gently pulled the tape from her mouth. She moaned, rubbing her sore arms.

"Are you all right?" Scott asked.

"I think so," Trudy said in a shaky voice. "He didn't really hurt me."

"Tell me what happened," he said.

"He took me by surprise," Trudy said. "He came up right behind me when I entered my apartment building. He said he was looking for a picture you had taken at the Mark Hopkins. I played dumb, Scott. I said I didn't know what he was talking about."

"It's a good thing you did," Scott said. He was thinking of the new negative he'd made.

"Come on," Scott said, "let's get out of here."

"What about the other pictures you took this morning?" Trudy asked, as they drove out of the park.

"All gone," Scott said. He told her what he had found when he got back to his apartment.

Trudy sighed. "So that's it! Our only clue is gone. You were right, Scott. Whatever happened in the gift shop was really important. And Jason must have been trying to tell you something. Do you still think 'blackbird' is someone's name?"

Scott nodded. "He's probably the same person who broke into my apartment and stole the pictures and negatives. And kidnapped you. But who is he and what is he really after? Jason said, 'Stop Blackbird.' Stop him from doing what?"

"Well, without that picture, we'll have a hard time figuring it out," Trudy said.

"Take it easy," Scott said. "I still have an ace up my sleeve." He told her about the copy he had made.

"Scott, that's great!"

"I took a big chance with your life," he told her. "If the kidnapper had figured out what I was really up to . . ."

"But he didn't," Trudy said. "Let's get over to your place right away and get a new print made."

When they got to Scott's apartment, he went right to work on the new negative. When the new print was ready, they studied it carefully. It showed Jason falling against the shelf. There was a small crowd of people near him. Some of the faces were unclear, and some of the people had their backs to the camera. But Scott recognized a few others. There was the woman in the yellow hat, and the businessman in the gray suit. The young newlyweds weren't looking at each other. For once they had something else to look at. And there was the tall soldier Scott had bumped into.

"Do any of those people look familiar?" Scott asked.

Trudy shook her head. "Not really, Scott. Besides, the man who kidnapped me had a stocking mask over his face. And he kept that hat and heavy coat on the whole time."

"Was there anything else you might have noticed?" Scott asked. "A scar or a tattoo?"

Trudy just shook her head again. "But there must be something about this picture this guy is afraid of," she said. "After all, he went to a lot of trouble to break in here and steal the prints and negatives."

Scott nodded his head in agreement. "He must have seen me snap those pictures this morning," Scott said slowly. "I guess he must have followed me around today to find out where I live. Then, after I left to meet you, he broke in here. He must have discovered that one of the pictures was missing by matching the prints and the negatives."

"How did he find out about me?" Trudy asked.

"I wrote our dinner date down on my desk calendar." Scott said. "He probably waited outside the restaurant and decided to follow you home. I guess he figured the best way to force me to hand over the picture was by threatening you."

Trudy sighed. "Well, all this still doesn't help us figure out the mystery, Scott. I guess we may have to wait till Jason comes to. Maybe he'll be able to tell us what happened. No one else knows what this is all about."

"We may not be able to wait," Scott said. "I have this funny feeling that we just don't have a lot of time to figure this thing out."

"Scott, do you think Jason is in danger?" Trudy said suddenly. "Do you think the kidnapper will go after *him?* After all, Jason knows something important."

"Right now Jason is in intensive care," Scott said. "There is always a nurse on duty. I don't think Blackbird or whoever he is, will be able to get to Jason very easily."

"What do you think really happened this morning?" Trudy said.

Scott frowned. "I've been trying to figure that out. You know, if Blackbird is a guest at the hotel, he must be from out of town. So he's come to the city for some reason."

"Jason must have recognized his voice," Trudy said. "They must have known each other at some time in the past. But I guess Blackbird didn't recognize Jason."

"Jason hasn't always had a beard." Scott said. "He told me once he grew it after his accident. It helped hide the scars. And now he always wears dark glasses."

"I'll bet Blackbird is someone Jason knew in the days when he worked for the CIA," Trudy said excitedly. "That gives me an idea. Why don't I contact some newspaper reporters I know tomorrow morning? A few of them work back in Washington. They might know something about 'Blackbird', and if he did once work for the CIA."

"Good idea," Scott said. "At this point we need some leads—and some luck."

When the alarm clock rang the next morning, Scott was tempted to shut if off and crawl back under the covers. But he had a busy day ahead of him. All the pictures he'd taken of the Mark Hopkins were gone. So he had to do the job all over again. And he still had other hotels to photograph. He gritted his teeth and climbed out of bed.

Scott worked hard all morning. He also called the hospital a few times to check on Jason's condition. But the answer was always the same. Jason was still unconscious. In one way that really worried Scott. But in another way, he was relieved. That meant Jason was still in intensive care, and Blackbird wouldn't be able to get to him.

It was early afternoon when Scott finally finished taking the pictures he needed. He headed back for his apartment to develop the rolls of film. The moment he unlocked his door, he heard the phone ringing. He ran to answer it. It was Trudy.

"Scott, I've been trying to call you for two hours," she said. "I found out about Blackbird."

Scott sucked his breath in sharply. "What did you find out?" he asked anxiously. "Did he work for the CIA?"

"Yes," Trudy said. Quickly she told him the whole story. "Blackbird" was the code name of an agent who had worked with Jason in the CIA. The two men had been partners in an important operation.

Eight years before, the CIA had learned that a political assassin from Europe had sneaked into the United States. They had learned that an enemy nation had hired the assassin to kill the president of the United States. Jason and Blackbird had been assigned to hunt down and capture the assassin. After weeks of detective work, and some good tips, the agents had tracked him down.

But someone had warned the assassin that Jason and Blackbird were after him. The agents thought they had cornered him in an old abandoned warehouse. But the assassin was ready for them. He had rigged up an explosion to kill them when they entered the building.

Then something went wrong. The explosion accidentally set the whole building on fire. Jason barely managed to escape. He was badly injured and blinded for life. The assassin and Blackbird were trapped in the fire. They both died.

When Trudy finished her story, Scott said, "So that's what happened! Jason never told me any of the details."

"There's more to the story," Trudy said. "Remember I told you that someone had warned the assassin that the CIA was after him?"

"Go on," Scott said.

"Afterward, they found out that it had been Blackbird. He was really a double agent—a spy for two countries. He was working for the CIA as well as the country that had hired the assassin."

"Jason must have been pretty bitter when he found out that his partner was a traitor."

"I'm sure he was!" Trudy said. "I guess that's why he never talks about it."

Scott was silent for a moment. Then he said, "Wait a minute. You said Blackbird died in the fire."

"That's right," Trudy said. "After the fire, they found the remains of two bodies. One was the body of the assassin."

"What about the other one?" Scott asked.

"It was burned beyond recognition. But they assumed it had to be Blackbird. He had disappeared, and he never was seen again."

"Trudy, don't you see?" Scott said, excitement rising in his voice. "The second body could have belonged to someone else. It could have been a street person living in that warehouse. It could have been anyone!"

"I don't know," Trudy said. "I guess you could be right."

"Or maybe Blackbird rigged the whole thing up to begin with," Scott said. "What if he killed someone and put the body in the warehouse to make it look like he had died in that fire."

"That makes sense," Trudy said. "And then he went into hiding. He probably thought he was pretty safe until Jason recognized his voice."

"So if Blackbird has been lying low all these years," Scott said, "why is he here now?"

"That's a good question," Trudy said. "And we're still going in circles. We don't know why he's in San Francisco. We don't even know what he looks like."

"And the photograph hasn't been much help," Scott said. "Unless—" He stopped.

"What is it?" Trudy asked.

"Maybe the desk clerk at the hotel could help us," Scott said. "Maybe he can tell us something about the guests in the picture. It wouldn't hurt to ask."

"I'll meet you at the hotel," Trudy said quickly.

When they both got to the Mark Hopkins, Scott showed the photo to the desk clerk. "Jason Roberts is a good friend of mine," he told the clerk. "I'm still trying to figure out what happened to him yesterday. I was hoping that one of these people might be able to tell me."

The clerk shrugged. "It seemed like just an accident to me," he said. "But I can tell you who the guests are." He studied the photo.

"This is Mr. Sanders," he said, pointing to the businessman in the gray suit. "He comes to San Francisco about three times a year on business. He's from Chicago."

Scott wrote down the information as the clerk talked.

"The lady in the hat is Mrs. Lundgren. She's a widow. Her children and grandchildren live in the city. The soldier is Sgt. Collins. He's on leave and visiting friends here. The young couple is on their honeymoon. I'll look up their names if you'll wait a minute."

While he was gone, Scott and Trudy looked at the photo.

"It could be Mr. Sanders," Scott said. "It could also be Sgt. Collins."

Trudy nodded. "I guess we can take Mrs. Lundgren and the honeymooners off the list," she said. "That narrows it down a bit."

Scott stared at the face of the young husband. "It's hard to tell just how old he is," Scott said. "If he's in his mid-thirties, he could be Blackbird."

"That's true," Trudy said. "And what a good cover that would make. Who would suspect a man who's supposed to be on his honeymoon?"

"We haven't narrowed the list down that much," Scott said.

The desk clerk returned shortly with the names of the young couple. Scott and Trudy thanked the man and walked off. "Do you really want to question all these people?" Trudy asked when they were outside.

"Well, I was thinking that if we heard the voice, maybe we would recognize Blackbird. On the other hand, that's dangerous. But I don't know what else we can do. We seem to be running out of—" He stopped, frowning at Trudy. She was staring at something a few feet away. "What is it?" Scott asked. "What do you see?"

"That's it!" she gasped. "Now I know why Blackbird came to San Francisco. I know who he's after, Scott!"

Trudy dashed over to a newspaper box and bought a copy of the morning paper. She hurried back to Scott. "Look," she said, "there's another article about Malcolm Carruthers. He's going to be giving his speech tonight at the Civic Center."

"So?" Scott asked.

"Well, don't you see?" Trudy said impatiently. "You were wondering what would bring Blackbird out of hiding. I bet Carruthers is Blackbird's target."

"Why?" Scott said. "What would Blackbird want with Carruthers?"

"Think about it," Trudy said. "Not everyone wants that war in the Middle East to end. What about the arms dealers? They would lose a lot of money if they had no one to sell weapons to. War is good business for them."

"That's true," Scott said, "but—"

"If Carruthers were to be assassinated, the war would probably start up again.

Each side would blame the other side for his death." Scott nodded. What Trudy said made sense. But for some reason, her idea didn't feel right to Scott. He had the feeling that there was something they had overlooked. Or maybe a piece of the puzzle was still missing.

"Well, don't just stand there," Trudy said, grabbing his hand. "We've got to get over to the Civic Center. Carruthers will be making his speech at Davies Auditorium. We have to find the people in charge of security and warn them. It's a good thing that Carruthers won't be speaking until tonight. We have plenty of time."

When they reached the Civic Center, Trudy jumped out of the car. Scott climbed out more slowly. "Hurry up," Trudy said.

"You go ahead," Scott told her. "I'll take a look at the auditorium. Meet you back here at the car."

Trudy nodded and hurried away. Scott walked slowly over to the auditorium. He saw that the building was already humming with activity. Everything was being set up for Carruthers' speech. Security was very tight. There were guards posted at every door.

Scott stopped to talk to one of the guards. He learned that a big crowd was expected. "But if anyone thinks he can slip into the auditorium and cause trouble, he's a fool!" the guard said. "We aren't taking any chances."

Trudy was waiting by the car when Scott returned. "I talked to the head of security," she said. "I told him everything we knew about Blackbird. He took it seriously and he said he'd look into the matter right away."

"Security is already very tight here," Scott said. "Blackbird doesn't stand a chance of killing Carruthers. Even an expert, paid assassin would . . ."

He stopped in mid-sentence. Suddenly Scott knew what had been bothering him. "That's it!" he cried. "Trudy, Carruthers isn't Blackbird's target!"

"He isn't?" Trudy said.

"I started to say that even an expert assassin would have a hard time killing Carruthers with so much tight security present. And that's the point, Trudy. Blackbird's *not* a paid assassin. He never was. He was a spy and a traitor, yes. But never a gun for hire. If someone wanted to hire a killer, I'm sure there are other men who are known to be paid assassins."

"Well, if what you say is true, then why is he here?" Trudy asked.

"I think he's after Alan Carter," Scott said.

"Carter?" Trudy said in surprise. "But why?"

"Because Carter's been promising to reveal secret information about a former CIA agent in his book. He says it's a man who turned out to be a double agent."

"Blackbird!" Trudy said.

"Right," Scott said. "Maybe Blackbird heard Carter's speech in another city. Maybe he read an article about Carter and the book he's writing. Those hints that Carter has been dropping probably scared him. He has no way of knowing how much or how little Carter knows. He may even think that Carter knows for sure that he's still alive."

"Carter is giving his speech today at San Francisco State," she said.

"What time?" Scott said, as they hurried toward her car.

"Look in the newspaper," Trudy said. "There's probably something about it in there."

Scott turned the pages as fast as he could. "I found it," he said finally. "Carter is due to speak in less than an hour."

"I don't know if we can get there in time," Trudy said. "The traffic is pretty heavy.

Maybe we should find a phone and call the school."

"No!" Scott said. "By the time we found someone to take our story seriously, it could be too late."

They both fell silent while Trudy wove her car in and out of traffic. Scott gritted his teeth, knowing there was no way she could go any faster. As they drove on, Scott wondered if they were jumping to conclusions about Carter being in danger. After all, what did Scott really know about spies, double agents, killers? He was a *photographer!*

Yet something told him he was right. He knew part of being a successful photographer was luck—being in the right place at the right time. And he couldn't help but feel he *had* been in the right place when he'd snapped those photos of Jason being injured.

It could be a *coincidence* that an ex-CIA agent and traitor, believed dead, would show up in San Francisco now. And at the same time, an ex-CIA agent promising to tell all in a new book would show up as well. It *could* be a coincidence, Scott knew. But, deep down, he also knew he didn't believe that for one moment.

Fifty minutes later Trudy parked her car near the curb in front of the university. "You go ahead," she told Scott. "Try to stop Blackbird if you can. I'll find a place to park and contact the campus guards."

Scott jumped out of the car and dashed across campus. Stop Blackbird! That was easier said than done. How could he stop Blackbird when he didn't even know what the man looked like?

The auditorium was just ahead. Groups of people were going in. Carter was due to begin his speech in a few minutes. Scott ran up the steps, taking them two at a time.

The crowd was larger that Scott had thought it would be. That would make it even harder to find Blackbird. Where would he sit? And who should Scott look for? Mr. Sanders, the Chicago businessman? Sgt. Collins, or the young husband? Or had Blackbird chosen a new disguise?

Scott felt a sense of despair. His task seemed hopeless. Then he realized that Blackbird wouldn't sit just anywhere. He would probably sit near an exit so he could make a quick escape.

Suddenly the lights on stage came up and the houselights dimmed. That was the signal to people in the audience to find seats. Scott pushed through the people still crowding the aisles. It was hard to make out faces of people at the back of the auditorium. Then Scott remembered that his telephoto lens was still attached to his camera. He pulled the camera out of the bag and put it to his eye. Faces in the distance came clearly into view.

On stage he heard someone come to the microphone. Alan Carter was introduced. The audience began to clap. Scott scanned the faces in each section of the auditorium. He was beginning to feel desperate. No one he saw looked familiar.

Suddenly, not 20 feet away, Scott saw a bright flash of color. A wide-brimmed yellow hat and a large purse! Scott focused his camera on the face. It was Mrs. Lundgren, the widow! What in the world— Scott saw her reach into her purse. She pulled out something small and dark. It was a gun!

Scott shouted and raced up the aisle. People around him looked startled. Scott quickly closed the gap between himself and Blackbird. But it wasn't good enough. Blackbird aimed at the stage. Thinking quickly, Scott raised the camera and pressed the button. Light from the flash attachment exploded in Blackbird's face. It was enough to blind the assassin for an instant. Scott threw himself at Blackbird, knocking him over. The gun flew out of his hand and slid across the floor.

Around them, people screamed and scattered. Scott tried to pin Blackbird to the floor, but the man was too strong. Scott felt Blackbird's hands close around his throat. Pain shot through him, and he gasped for breath. Suddenly, several campus guards pulled the killer off of him. Scott took a deep breath, and drew air into his lungs.

"Scott! Are you all right?" He looked up into Trudy's worried face. He managed a weak nod and a grin.

Trudy helped Scott to his feet. The first thing he reached for was his camera. Luckily it had not been damaged in the fight.

The guards were starting to take Blackbird away. For the first time Scott got a good look at the traitor. The hat and woman's wig had fallen off in the fight. Without his disguise, Blackbird looked very different. His eyes were filled with hatred. "I should have killed you two when I had the chance," he said.

Scott raised his camera and shot a picture of Blackbird. He knew that when the film was developed, he would have a picture of a cold-blooded killer, a picture of evil. He shivered a little when he thought of how close Blackbird had come to killing him.

Later, after Scott and Trudy had given their statements to the police, Scott called the hospital. Finally, the news was good. Jason had come to. Scott and Trudy hurried over to the hospital to see him. He was still very weak and the nurse told them they couldn't stay long. But they had enough time to let Jason know that Blackbird had been captured.

After he heard Scott's story, Jason smiled weakly. "That is good news, Scott. When I heard his voice in the shop, I could hardly believe my ears. What a horrible shock! It was like hearing a voice from the grave!"

Scott laughed. "He was probably trying out his disguise, trying to get used to it in public before wearing it on the day he planned to kill Carter. He shouldn't have worn that wide-brimmed hat. That's what got him into trouble."

"That's right," Jason said. "I heard something fall off a shelf and then I heard Blackbird curse. He forgot for a moment that he was supposed to be a woman. He spoke in his normal voice, a voice I thought I'd only hear in my nightmares.

"I'm glad Blackbird has finally been captured," Jason went on. "But more than anything else, I'm just glad you two are all right."

Trudy smiled. "So are we, Jason. Capturing traitors is *not* the kind of work Scott and I have been trained for."

Scott nodded and then laughed. "Speaking of capturing . . ." he said. "I better get back to capturing some of San Francisco's finest hotels on film. It may not be very exciting, but after the last few days, it suits me just fine."